HOW TO BEAT THE SHARKS WHEN THE WATER'S POLLUTED

Or How To Succeed In Sales When Your Product Stinks

MIKE SEVENAU

Copyright © 1997

All rights reserved. No part of this book may be reproduced in any form, except for the inclusion of brief quotations in a review, without permission in writing from the author or publisher.

Published by M.G. Publishing
San Francisco, California

Second Printing • 2000 • May 1997

Library of Congress Catalog Card Number: 97-91592

ISBN 1-57502-445-4

Additional copies may be obtained by sending in the order form found at the back of this book with a check.

Printed in the USA by
Mooris Publishing
3213 E. Hwy 30
Kearny, NE 68847
800-650-7888

This book is dedicated to my wife Becky.

You were <u>so</u> patient when daily, all I could talk about was "the" book. But most of all, I dearly appreciate your loyalty, your trust in me, and your intense love for your little family... Thank you!

ACKNOWLEDGEMENTS

I would like to thank two people, without whose efforts this book would not have been possible. First, the Graphic Artist responsible for all of the illustrations, Chris Williams, and second, the one who transcribed my notes and tapes into manuscript form, Ted Johnson. Thanks to both of you.

Also, I can't forget Steve Marini for his support, Keith Videtto who was very encouraging, Richard Nolan M.D. for his advice, and Terrie Johnson for her "in-betweens".

"Finally, thanks to my late father Lou who taught me how to fish without bait."

CONTENTS

Chapter 1 . . . . . The First Days
Chapter 2 . . . . . You!
Chapter 3 . . . . . Ask Questions, Perform Dialog Selling
Chapter 4 . . . . . Ethics – Simple, Have Them!
Chapter 5 . . . . . Insecurity – A Huge Blessing – Take It to the Bank and Cash In On It!
Chapter 6 . . . . . Organized For Success
Chapter 7 . . . . Salesperson – No. Consultant – Yes.
Chapter 8 . . . . . Know Your Competition
Chapter 9 . . . . . Listen, Stupid!!
Chapter 10 . . . . What About Home?
Chapter 11 . . . . Early Bird, Catch That Worm!
Chapter 12 . . . . You're On the Inside!
Chapter 13 . . . . Feed Your Family, Not Your Ego!
Chapter 14 . . . . Thank You!
Chapter 15 . . . . Walk In Backwards
Chapter 16 . . . . Do It Now!
Chapter 17 . . . Sales Meetings: Bane or Boom?
Chapter 18 . . . . Motivate, Motivate, Motivate!
Chapter 19 . . . . You Lose! What's Next?
Chapter 20 . . . . The Last Word!

INTRODUCTION

Anyone and everyone can have some measure of success selling a product that is wonderful and really works! Most of us are told very early in our sales careers that if you believe in your product and apply yourself diligently, huge sales commission checks are right around the corner.

But what about the thousands of sales people who have to sell a product that is marginal at best? What about those of us who know, without a doubt, that our product just doesn't work? Yet, we still have to sell it, don't we? Is there any hope? Or do these unfortunate scourges of the sales world have to tread water financially until a good sales job comes along highlighting a product that is sound?

Don't throw in the towel!! Help is on the way. Do you hear the cavalry horns sounding? There's real hope for all!! Yes, you too can be very, very successful selling a product that has holes in it! If you apply the suggestions in this book, you can sell anything to anyone at anytime! Yes, you can beat the sharks when you should be their dinner. I did, and you can too.

CHAPTER ONE - THE FIRST DAYS

This job is it! It's the exact position you have been looking for! Life is good. Everything looks cleaner, roses smell more pungent and darn it, this time you're gonna make it big! Get out of my way or you'll get run over by my personal sales train! Choo-choo, choo-choo. Chug-lug-lug-lug. Chug-lug-lug-lug. It seems they've given you a relatively high commission rate with the freedom to explore the limits within your gold mine of a territory. (One time I had a general manager tell me he was sending me into the mother lode to pan for gold. Gold that was dropping out of the trees and into your pan. All I had to do was catch it. What a crock!!).

There is very little office time with only a pager tying you to your gold digging boss. The turnover ratio bothers you some but that was other lazy salespeople, not you. And they just couldn't deliver the goods, plain and simple. You're different!!

However, after a few days in the field, suspicions start to surface. Maybe it was that door slamming in your friendly, smiling face. Or perhaps it was the hatred for your product that some seemed to have! But the last straw was delivered when someone had the temerity to hold you personally responsible for the money he had wasted by using your company. Wow, what a letdown! Suspicion has turned into an ugly reality. You know what? My product stinks! Oh no!

Frankly, most at this point think of pulling in their reins. Yes, our sales antennas go up and the signals we're getting are fuzzy at best. The boss still claims the product is the end-all. But we all know better. And plus, he doesn't have to sell it. (Lucky lug!) He says he's as good a salesman as you are, you know. (Ha ha). On second thought there was that salary position in the office that was offered to you. The money was guaranteed and it's yours if you can't stand the heat in the field. Or better yet, maybe you should keep this job doing just enough to get by until something better comes along. There is that guarantee that lasts for a couple of months. What do I do? Decisions, decisions, decisions.

You know what? It's only natural for someone not to want to expend a lot of energy on something that's not going pay off down the line. But it's at this point (drum roll please....) that the real sales people surface and the pretenders go back to stocking shelves and emptying garbage cans. There is more than hope. There is a guarantee that this sales gig can end up making you a legend in your own time. It did for me. How?

That's a good question that I'm going to spend the rest of this book answering to the best of my ability. Trust me, this is great stuff that has taken me over thirty years of sales dominance to acquire. And for the lousy cover price of this paperback you're going to get a lifetime of sales tips. But more important than that, you will acquire a sales philosophy! You'll be able to develop a mind set that is worth more to a salesperson than that literal pot of gold. With my help and if you pay rapt attention, you will develop some-

thing that very few people have. The ability to make a lot of money. Hang in there with me. Turn to the next page. You won't be sorry!

CHAPTER TWO - YOU!

Now that I've used my considerable sales skills to interest you in reading further, I'd better give you something you can take to the bank to cash in. Yes, I'd better put up or shut up or I could lose you! You'll close the book and never open it again unless I deliver something now!!

So here it goes.....
Pay attention to this one! It seems that when we sell anything, we have to remember that the golden rule, the first rule of thumb, is to sell yourself. You'd be surprised how basic this is but how much it is forgotten out in the field. You get so hung up on the advantages of the product, the client's needs, the prices, product knowledge and so on, that you forget to sell the most important commodity, you! <u>You are it!</u>

Let me explain. We need our clients to think so highly of us that it reflects on our product. To translate into understandable sales talk, our customer should think that this product must work because we are hawking it! Answer this question, you doubting Thomas, what super successful salesperson would ever have a relationship with a lousy product? Yep, you've got it - none!! A super sales person could work for anyone he wants, so therefore logic dictates that he would only work for the ultimate product or company. So even if our product isn't the best, it doesn't prevent us from being the finest salesmen on the face of this earth. And if we are perceived as such, we've taken the most important step in selling a product that isn't as good as our boss says it is.

> • **STEP NUMBER ONE**
> Sell yourself as the best salesperson in the universe and your product will only be seen in that context....

Now reason on this fact. If you're a great salesperson, you know what, you are in demand! Whether you know it or not (and you should by now), you are worth buying stocks in. You're a wonderful commodity. Usually one in your position calls his or her own shots as far as employment is concerned. The key here is to take that mind set (being number one) and immediately apply it to yourself and your territory. Start thinking you are the best and darn it, you will be - guaranteed! Now since you are numero uno, your customers will see your confidence and esprit de corps and reward you with respect and dignity and big orders, (most important part) being the tops in your field deserves. See how easy that was?! Think you are the best, and you will be. And believe it or not, your customers will hitch their wagons to your team of horses. Where you go, they will follow. Even if it is to another company. Everyone loves a winner! Never lose this attitude.

> • **STEP NUMBER TWO**
> Think you are the best and you will be!!

Obviously, there are times out in the trenches that we have to feed our families rather than our egos. But never surrender your status as the best! When you introduce yourself to a client, make sure he or she knows of your status as top dog. Remind him continuously by sharing sales awards, talking up bonuses, thanking them always for keeping you on top. One year when I was named Salesperson of the Year and given a nice write-up and trophy, I took those platitudes on the road with me and shared them with all my customers. I even have pictures taken with them (my customers) standing next to me with my award. Why? Because first I was thanking them for helping me to achieve this honor. And second, I was reaffirming my status as the best! If you take pictures, make sure you develop the photos and bring them back mounted so they can hang them in their offices. I guarantee you they will be hung up and each business day most of your clients will be reminded continuously of their close relationship with you and your status. It's like having an advertisement of your greatness in each of your sales stops. And tell me, oh "Swami of Sales", when money gets tight and someone is sent packing down the road, who do you think it's going to be? Someone on the wall who is like family or that new fellow who always seems to be in a hurry to get to his next stop?

That brings us nicely to the next point. Take your <u>time</u> with your customer. Absolutely no one likes to be rushed. It devalues your relationship with a client much faster than your product not pulling its own weight. What you are telling your customer by hurrying is that he is not important enough to spend time with. You also are telling him that you take him for granted. You got him so you're off to conquer new worlds. Don't do it! Make each customer feel that he is your closest friend and best account. Even if they are small potatoes, treat them right and the business will grow. Referrals will magically appear. And while you are at it, don't just fuss over the one giving you the order. Make it your business to get to know everyone at this establishment. But hold on a minute, you say. That's impossible! That would take too much time and plus, most sales managers tell us to get to the decision maker and don't waste time anywhere else. Yes, we've all heard stories about the poor sap who called on the wrong person for six months and finally found out that he wasn't the one who had the authority to give him the business. I'm not talking about that! That's common sense. But you know what; If you make everyone your friend, they will tell you who you need to see. Don't be afraid to ask someone on the floor about his boss, his family, his job and if he's happy and most importantly if there's anything you can do for him!. This is what makes you unique. Not only do you care about all people who have to sell your product, but you get nice inside scoops on the boss and the business which you use to your advantage in cementing your relationship with your customer.

Here is an interesting example of this plan put into action! Once, out in the field, we called on a car dealership, one of my salesmen and yours truly. My guy asked for a particular manager and was told he was off that day. Then he gave a copy of our latest work to the salesman and asked if he would make sure Mr. So-and-So got it. Now he was ready to leave and slay the next dragon. But we had driven there, so I was going to at least get my money's worth. I told the salesman at the dealership (who had a unique voice) that he sounded familiar, that somehow I knew him. He was happy with the attention that he was getting and replied happily that everyone gets him confused with Wolfman Jack and that he had done some radio.

Wow, I was impressed and explained that I was the sales manager and that I listened to the station he appeared on. We talked for awhile and after we got chummy we shared some common interests in the business. Now remember, this was just a salesman on the floor of the establishment. A nobody in most people's eyes. I asked him how he would approach Mr. Boss to get on his good side. I'll be darned if he didn't spill the beans on the whole operation. You see, Mr. Boss wasn't the one who really handled the order giving. He was the setup to take the heat off the real decision maker because he was already much too busy. So my guy had been calling on the wrong person for months. But now we had to strike while the iron was hot! "Tell me Mr. Wolfman, how do I get in to see Mr. Order-giver?" "Well that's impossible" he explained, "but if you show up on Friday morning, that's when he writes all his orders and you might be able to impress him". Great. Now I've got some real information. But you know what? The great ones don't stop there. You've got a cow giving you milk. Don't stop until the udders are empty! I continued, "So tell me, if you showed up on Friday, how would you approach him? Does he like wine? Is he all business? How about coffee?" Now we're cooking!! (I can smell a tasty sale!) And finally, our friend tells us that the way to this particular gentleman's heart is his family. He loves them and is trying to build a future for them. Great. Now I've got a hot button.

So on Friday I take my five year old by the dealership in my family wagon and stop by to introduce myself. My kid is with me because I felt she should share a work morning with her dad, the best in the business. Now you tell me oh Sales Guru, what do

you think happened there?! Yep, you're right, another lucky score for the guy who makes things happen. All because I took the time to talk to someone who had no authority or clout. The other nice thing is that before I left (with my huge order, of course), I reaffirmed my relationship with Mr. Wolfman and told him I owed him and I would find some special way of rewarding him in the future. The only hitch was, I needed to catch on here. So I told Wolfman if I was still writing business next month, tickets to the 49ers would be his. I wonder who got noticed the next month? Yep, that's right. And remember, we haven't talked about the product working, we've just taken advantage of a simple rule of sales. The "WIIFM" theory. What's In It For Me? If we allow all people that we touch to win, regardless of their position, we'll be writing business in the deepest of recessions and at the best of times too! Of course, that means we've got to get into other people's heads, doesn't it? We can't be totally consumed with ourselves! We don't count. The order we want to write doesn't count. The only important variable here is what makes our customers tick and putting a smile on their face!

I remember hearing a story about a thing called Samurai Selling and it stuck with me for all these years. It kind of goes like this:

The Samurai were a group of individuals who were the servants of the Warlord. Most think Samurai were aggressive, physical soldiers, but they weren't. They were cerebral and, if needed, they could obviously protect their master. Their main objective was to know their boss so well that they knew what he needed before he needed it. Imagine that! After observing, serving, observing some more and watching every move of their master, after a number of years, the Samurai could basically read his Warlord's mind. The Japanese have a word, "tengishi", for the co-mingling of your mind with someone else. It's making their thoughts yours! After some time, the harmony between the two was established and heck, the big guy didn't even have to ask for a glass of water anymore. His Samurai knew he needed one before he did. In battle it was the same. Now notice, the Warlord was the guy that got all the press clippings. When the battle was won, he was adorned with rewards, and awards from the King. But how about his sidekick, the Samurai? Don't worry. Those who served as Samurai were rewarded with beautiful living accommodations, lots of money (yen), gorgeous geisha girls and whatever their hearts desired. Why? Because they sublimated their ego and served their master! It was said that no one except the King and Warlords lived better than our Samurai friends.

Now let's apply this! You see, we in the field find ourselves in the very same position. For we're not the King, who is basically the one who owns the company. We're not the Warlord who is the sales manager. But yet, if we practice getting into our customers heads and knowing what they need before they even know it themselves, we will certainly have the same rewards or even more!

It's a good rule of thumb, that a good salesman always makes more than his sales manager. That's why the great ones never manage. Don't be tempted by the power or position or even the security. If you are good at what you do, stick with it! Most will

agree that just because you are good in selling doesn't mean you are good at managing. I say amen to that. But you ask, how do I get inside my customer's head? How do I get to know him so well that I know his needs before even he does?

Keep on going! You can't stop now!

CHAPTER THREE - ASK QUESTIONS, PERFORM DIALOG SELLING

Especially true with a product that stinks, we have to know everything we can about our customer. Without the use of questions, we could never learn anything in life as well as sales. Learn something new every time you talk to them. And then most importantly, write down what you've learned. Don't trust the old memory. Remember, we forget a lot more than we retain! Pretty soon if you review your notes and make meshing with your order taker a priority I guarantee you'll hear those awesome inspiring words, "How did you know I needed to do that? I was just thinking about doing something along those lines. You're good!" Believe me when you hear those spine tingling words, you're on your way to achieving true sales greatness. Make it a priority to pick out one customer at a time if you're just starting, and form that bond. Notice I used the word bond. That's a strong simile isn't it? Sounds like you're marrying someone, huh? But it's what you want with all your customers, "a bond". If you've achieved a bond, loyalty to you and your product will be right around the corner. Now, no one can waltz in and steal your client. Why? Because you have a <u>bond</u> together and if anything, that's even more appreciated when the other sales guys come in with no knowledge of their customer and they try to ramrod whatever they are pushing that week.

Once I had a customer ask me if I had just read a magazine article in *Success* magazine. I hadn't gotten mine yet but he said that a famous older salesman had advised that all salesmen do what I had been doing for him for months. Is that where I got my ideas? No, I exclaimed, I was born with my customer's best interests at heart. I care about them plain and simple!! He told me it shows and gave me a huge order. But at the same time he remarked that he had skipped breakfast and hoped he could make it through the day. It took me exactly 12 minutes to get back to him with a breakfast of bagels and cream cheese and lox with cafe mocha and the works. You see what he didn't tell me was that he wished someone would get him something. He didn't even know he wanted that himself! But I knew it, acted on it and I swear I noticed a little tear forming in his eye when I personally delivered his meal. Now tell me, when he is hit all day long by other salesmen with a product as good or better than mine, who wins? Yes indeed, the Sales Samurai. Who cashes the biggest checks? Yes again, the Sales Samurai. Do it! Get into your customers heads, know what they need and the trust and bond you make with them will last forever.

CHAPTER FOUR - ETHICS - SIMPLE, HAVE THEM!

I'm certainly not one to preach about morality. Ethics for our discussion are simply sales ethics. What you do at night or on the weekends is your business. But know this, if you party all night, get very little sleep, and have a headache when you start your sales day, I guarantee you, this isn't going to be one of your finest hours. You'll have to gut it out of course, but better yet, show respect for your body and it will pay you dividends! If you want to be the best, consider yourself in sales training. If you have a big day planned the next day, get home early and get your needed rest. Not only will you physically be ready for a great day but more importantly, mentally you'll be on top of your game! Think for a second, which spells success? Paying attention to that ear-splitting headache, coping with nausea, or devising methods for interesting your client in your product. Remember, we're all human and take the course of least resistance, and even if you make your designated calls for the day you'll go home as early as possible when you're not feeling well. I always have a clear head ready for sales war! Who do you think has the best chance of succeeding, the vibrant , happy, bouncing off the walls salesperson, or the sweating, withdrawn, pale soldier who obviously is not at his best? See yourself as the customer sees you. They aren't stupid, they know when you're trying to pull the wool over their eyes. Once with a hangover is acceptable, but more than once gives them the idea that perhaps this is an everyday occurrence. And tell me who would you trust, the party guy or Mike, the stable one, who always means business? It's an obvious answer, isn't it?

Let's move on. I recall one sales meeting I was talking about aggressive sales attitudes. Quickly I was corrected by one of our sales gals, that it was assertive, not aggressive, behavior that was needed. I humbly gave in to her but now I've changed my mind. Aggressiveness is what the best eat for lunch! It's a mind set. Aggressive people are always assertive but assertive ones aren't always aggressive. To illustrate, let's think of a lion stuck in an area of the forest where there is little to eat. Anything that moves catches his alert eye. Why? Simple, Bwana, because his survival depends on his ability to catch his dinner. A leaf falls and he aggressively attacks! Nuts, just a leaf! But a bush rustles a hint and he's on that too and guess what? A rodent was hiding underneath. A hungry, aggressive lion misses nothing and the best salesperson working with a sub par product has to be the same! Be aggressive, pursue everything as if your life depends on it! You can't afford to do anything but! Attractive game is not plentiful in our line of work. When you meet the good ones in our business you can see the aggressive attitude in their eyes can't you? It's amazing, the strong really do survive. If you go back to the lion example, ask yourself, why didn't he take note of the bush moving a tad and record it in his memory and save the information for later? Because he couldn't! Another lion at any time could beat him to his catch or the rodent could have dug a hole and escaped. So it was incumbent on the king of the jungle to spring into action or lose his chance. Certainly we are also in a position of competing with others for our food. If we don't strike while

the iron is hot, you'll lose guaranteed! Our customer will be contacted by another more aggressive salesperson, his needs will change or he'll spend his money on something else. Never put off that call on your potential customer. Never falsely reason, "Oh, he'll be there tomorrow. He knows I'll be there soon so there's no urgency." Don't say, "I'm tired, I want to go home." Just don't do it!!! Sales karma dictates that when you skip that call someone else will make it for you and you'll have lost your opportunity.

What does this have to do with ethics, you ask? Good question. You see, when one talks about aggressive behavior there's a fine line between aggressive good behavior, forcing the issue and that of being unethical. Be careful here. Always remain ethical in all you do! Never promise anything you can't deliver, never talk bad about your competition, never ever cheat anyone! It will always catch up with you. We are in it for the long run and that kind of behavior will never ever pay off down the road! Plus you'll live a life of a thousand deaths. Every time you're paged or called by a customer that you've kinked, you'll be afraid that you have been caught. That's no way to live and certainly no way to build lasting relationships. While we're on the subject, avoid off-color jokes. They will lose you more than you will ever gain! Remain classy and ethical and you'll always retain the respect and admiration of all your clients.

Now, how about the ethical treatment of your fellow salespeople in the same company? Good question, huh? Personally I have always considered my fellow sales representatives enemies. What? How can you say that Mike? I'm being very honest here. Come

on, you're all competing for a piece of the pie. Don't be fooled. It's every man/woman for themselves!! I'll tell you why.

You see, I made the mistake of taking the job of sales manager one time. (Never do it. Sales managers don't make enough money and their lack of security is infamous.) Anyway it was a rather new company so they needed someone with experience to build it and to help the crew develop. So I tried to help all my colleagues. It was good for them because I was telling them sales secrets that took years for me to develop. And it was good for me (I thought) because it it's always better to give than to receive. WRONG! Salespeople are sharks. It's a dog-eat-dog world out there and most, like 99%, only care about what affects them! Here's one place in life that you don't make the mistake of being generous.

I'll give you an example. Like I said, I was involved in this start-up company, so I thought we were building something that would take care of me for the rest of my life. Part of my responsibilities were helping the new ones get acclimated to our special type of <u>market.</u> I thought I did my job well. And since I got a little percentage of what came in, I reasoned that after years of keeping my sales jewels to myself it was time to be the hero and help everyone. Questions were plentiful and I even worked with most of my cohorts in the field. Once I even established a territory on my own so the guy who was hired for it would have some business to start with. It became very commonplace to page me during a close or even when anyone was opening an account for that matter, because the help I gave was very useful. Either I knew the customers already, or found a way to find out interesting little tidbits of useful information and remember, at the same time I was running my own territory too!

A few months passed and the owner of the company said he wanted to talk to me! Great! I figured I was going to get a pat on the back or better yet a nice bonus check for being number one in sales along with being a very capable sales manager. You know, I even went out with the reps and started lots of accounts for them, daily cold calling by myself, and then just handing them over. Boy was I in for a shock. It seems that my boss was interested in how the team viewed me. That's natural and expected. But what was unexpected was their response. None of them ever gave me credit for a thing! They said I had a good sales pitch, but theirs was different and more applicable to their territory. For all the accounts I started and secrets I shared I got nothing! That's right, the large donut hole. My feelings were hurt badly, but as I reasoned months later, what else could I have expected?

Every salesperson's job is on the line. He or she has to put up or shut up. If something drops in their laps through someone else's effort or if things work out they always take 100% of the credit. It's the nature of the business. None of us would do anything to weaken our position in our company would we? No way! And by giving me my due credit for being Mr. Wonderful the reps would have actually been putting themselves in a very precarious position. Who needs a rep if the sales manager is the one doing the work? I had one guy who said that yes his numbers were down but that he had done everything himself! No one ever helped him and he felt all alone in the territory. He even went so far as accusing the boss of misleading him into thinking that everyone was going to help him achieve success. But yet whenever a close became difficult his number appeared magically in my pager.

To be honest I deserve exactly what I got (a kick to the groin) because each time I helped someone I got my ego massaged! A good rule of thumb for a great salesperson to remember is if your ego is being <u>massaged</u>, cut and run! You lose! Something's definitely wrong!! Massage your checkbook and take care of your own ego, because I guarantee that if someone is building you up, they will eventually tear you down. And that's no fun!

It seems like the joke was really on me with this company. We built it from a lousy ten page publication to close to 70 pages in a year. Sales were up over 150%. At the yearly dinner I was expecting two awards, one for being top salesman of the year and the other for being so generous with my knowledge as sales manager. No one did what I did nor could they! But my reward was the proverbial donut hole again and in four months the company was sold to a very large corporation.

The moral of the story is this. Never help anyone! No one appreciates a thing you do for them and you're only helping someone to beat you! It's not a pretty sight when you're held responsible for losing your share of the top spot, when in reality you've helped someone else to achieve it. I've never heard one salesman get up at an awards banquet and give credit to another salesman or sales manager for his or her success. This would be sales suicide. And it's just not done in our game. Keep your secrets and leads to yourself. If you do anything, throw your sales associates off the right track with misleading information. There, I said it. A lot of people are probably going to be mad at me for telling you this. But it's the truth. Help no one but yourself. Remember part of your sales psychology is being number one and telling everyone that you're the best and unfortunately, that goes away rather quickly if you share the wealth.

Of course every sales manager will argue with this notion and I don't blame them. They are interested in everybody's sales totals going up and up and up, not just yours. What you should be interested in is keeping as large a cushion as possible between you and the next salesperson in line. If you're writing 70% of the business and five other salesmen are writing 30% between them, your wish is the hierarchy's command. So why weaken your position with the boss by helping your sales comrades? It's war baby, inside the office as well as outside. Win the war with your associates and you'll always have a strong place in your company. Fight tooth and nail for everything. It's the truth, sad as it is, but one that will enable you to be on top and stay on top. Also gang, remember we are selling a product that is weak! If you're the only one having success selling it, it's you and not the product that gets the credit. If everyone is having a great time selling it, then the product gets the kudos, not you!

This reminds me of another related experience. You see I was the top producer in my first sales company for over five years. I wrote 40% of the business and was very stable in holding my numbers. I accomplished this even though the product stunk! One day, it seemed that management felt they needed to inspire the troops, so they came up with a rather effective plan (for them). You see, I was used to winning monthly awards and perks. These ranged from fresh turkeys, to wine train excursions, and AM/FM radios. I figured I had earned these and they were part of my fringe benefits. However, one awards banquet I received a plaque with the title "Mike Sevenau's Hall of Fame Award". It was to be hung in our home office in a place that all could see. A deserving salesperson would be honored each month by having his name engraved on the plaque. The wording was enough to pump my ego as large as a balloon. Now let's be honest, I should have followed my own advice on ego massaging and fought it. Why? C'mon, it's simple friends, I never got another award again. I had made history by having an award named after me but the perks stopped! I should have fought it but I didn't!

Never let them take away your perks, friends, because by allowing management that inroad, it won't be long before they try to cut your salary. Give in once, and you will always regret it! Now tell me, how did I gain anything when other salespeople were enjoying the dinners and listening to the AM/FM radios that I used to win? That's right, I didn't and it's just another example of what I've been talking about. It's war, and our enemies are inside our walls, as well as outside! No one else will tell you this because it doesn't have a pretty ring to it. But neither does selling a product that doesn't work. If life was fair, we would all be born into money instead of hav-

Ethics – Simple, Have Them!

ing to earn it!

NEVER HELP A SALES ASSOCIATE OR YOU MAY BE CREATING YOUR OWN PERSONAL FRANKENSTEIN MONSTER....IT'S SAD BUT TRUE....

CHAPTER FIVE INSECURITY - A HUGE BLESSING. TAKE IT TO THE BANK AND CASH IN ON IT!

Come on now, insecurity is good? For a sales person? No way you say!! But let's face it fellow sales psychos, all of us are full of insecurities. Even when we have success our thoughts gravitate to what we haven't accomplished.

I had one of my best friends in the game always come in with very high numbers. And you know, he was never satisfied! His words kept ringing in my ears; "Yeah, I did $12K but Mr. So-and-So and Joe Blow didn't run. Just think what I would have done if Mr. and Mrs. S. didn't skip this week." Now there's an insecure salesman! He had a great week but still focused on what could have been. I say nothing is wrong with that! He's not satisfied period! Just think how he'd be crying if he had a bad week. But you know what, that won't happen because his bad weeks are others records. I know its true for him, as well as myself, that somehow we feel we don't deserve our success. We're not that good! It wasn't that hard! Hey, I'm not bleeding!

Now obviously this short primer on being a great salesman with a lousy product doesn't allow us to go into the psychology of why some of us are the way we are. Maybe our parents didn't pat us on the head when we did something right. Or worse yet maybe our mom and dad compared us unfavorably to our older brothers and sisters. Whatever the case, let's face it, all of us carry emotional baggage from the past. Every one of us has intense feelings of insecurity. And I'm here to tell you that if you have these feelings, you have a great gift.

To prove my point ask yourself which attitude stifles success. The person who is always striving, never satisfied, or the smug I feel good about myself and don't need to change a thing type B personality? Right again sales professor, and a key point to understand here is that for someone to be the best he/she has to have some insecurities gnawing away at them. If they didn't then they'd be satisfied (bad word) with themselves and not open to improvement! So, the curse of insecurity is a huge <u>blessing!!</u> Take it to the bank and cash it every chance you have.

Think about it, you wouldn't have bought this great little book if you felt there was no room to improve. And believe me, in the sales game change is the order of the day. We as the best, have to be <u>constantly</u> changing and adjusting our presentation to our customers needs. If we don't, it becomes old hat to them and most importantly, dated to us. So in a constantly changing environment who do you think has the best chance of succeeding? The smug I don't need to change anything type? The one who says I don't need to go out of my way for anyone because I'm fine the way I am? You know them as the sales person who thinks, since his or her territory is established it's time to pull in the reins and coast for awhile. And of course they maintain the infamous sales attitude right out of the losers almanac, "They owe me a living, I did the dirty work, I made all those cold calls, now I'm done with that stuff. I can relax. I'm established!" Are any of these winning attitudes? I say no.

But here's a winning attitude and it's one that comes from someone who is insecure. Please notice the difference. This one spells success! Stop and listen to these golden sayings..."I need to make an extra call or two today to feel good about myself. No one owes me a living. I'm fortunate to be in the position I'm in, so I'm going to work real hard to stay here. I'm going to do whatever it takes to keep myself on top. I'll put as much distance between me and my sales comrades as possible! Since I'm not sure of myself, I'm going to give myself a new hobby, acquiring sales knowledge! I'll read every book I can get my hands on and try to get at least one new point from everything I read.

Notice I said at least one new point. You can consider it a victory if you read a book or a sales article and get that one point. But the trick is, write that point down or else you'll forget it. Keep a log of all the good sales points. Make something like an instruction manual for yourself. This can be used as a device to lift your spirits up in case you've had a bad day. It can even help you keep track of the great moments in your sales career. Like the time you sold someone who didn't want to be sold. Or even the time that you hit your biggest numbers. Or the moment that you got someone who said no and then sold them a gigantic order! So keep a log, keep a notebook and put all the things you learn in it. And also keep all your great memories in it. Kind of like a sales scrapbook.

Did I make my point? Who would you bet on? It wouldn't even be close, would it? One, Mr. Type-B is doomed to mediocrity, while Mr. Insecure is destined for the top. So don't feel that insecurity is anything but a blessing! Yes, sometimes when you are cold calling or trying to close a deal it rears its ugly little head, but cheer up, you can harness it, and let it bring you places you never dreamed possible. I've never met anyone on top who wasn't insecure. Have you? Look at all the famous figures in history. Napoleon, Howard Hughes (the richest man in the world), Malcolm Forbes, Ted Turner, I could go on and on. But they all had the drive and <u>insecurities</u> to get to the top and stay there! If you're not insecure in the least you'd better check your pulse, because you're probably not living. But turn that perceived negative into a wonderful positive. Did I make my point? Use that personality flaw to your advantage. Every time you feel it gnawing away at you thank God for it! This is one of the key ingredients to getting you on top and keeping you there. Remember those of us in this position cash the biggest checks by far. So, <u>give me insecurity or give me sales death!!</u> A little insecurity sure does make the good ones great and the great ones last. You control your own destiny and you call the shots.

THE CURSE OF INSECURITY IS A HUGE BLESSING.
   And speaking of insecure, most in sales seem to worry about their paychecks. Now unless your company has pulled the wool over your eyes and held a carrot in front of you that can never be reached (in that case look for a new place to hang your hat!) DON'T WORRY ABOUT MONEY! Boy that's a strange statement isn't it? But it's true! If you follow the steps and suggestions outlined in this book and others, work hard and smart, THE MONEY WILL

ALWAYS BE THERE!

You should only worry about making that extra call a day. Extend some effort collecting an overdue bill. Think about what method you can use to increase your sales, but don't waste your energy or creative thought processes on the almighty dollar. Why? Because if you're good and you take care of business, and become the best you can be, the money will always be there! It's always there for the best!! It's always there for the good ones too! Why?

It's simple, if your particular company doesn't pay well, you wouldn't be there. Think about the money when you sign up, not after you're there. And if cuts in commissions or sales territories happen, let's be honest, since you are the wonderful one, you have the power to move on. Don't worry though, because 95% of the time you've proven your value to your company and they won't let you go. They will have to find a way to accommodate their star. Just keep your sales up and the rest takes care of itself.

I'm sure you've all heard of the 20/80% factor. Simply put this is a golden rule of sales management. It states that 20% of your sales force writes 80% of the business. Now put your thinking cap on, sales scholar, if you are part of that 20%, do you really think they'd lose you? Hardly, unless they're idiots, and in that case it's good you found out now. You're their race horse, make sure you're eating the best and most hay.

Now, in working with so many salespersons in my career I have found that some spend time out in the

field computing how much they have made, or how big their next paycheck is going to be. Let's face it, we all pay attention to our paychecks, but there is a difference between casually paying attention, and making that check your focal point. If your check is the only thing that motivates you, <u>change quickly!</u> Motivate yourself to be the best! Read books, go to seminars, listen to tapes, be a student of sales. Stay out there for those final three or four calls and the money will always be there. But if you only worry about the money and devise ways of increasing it, you won't be creating a great sales person.

Let's put it another way. If you are interested in racing and have a superb race car, do you spend all of your time shining the exterior? Or do you wrench under the hood to make sure the engine is working to its optimum level? Which one will win the race? It's rather obvious isn't it? And it's the same with you bean counters out there. DON'T, and I repeat DON'T, count nickels because I guarantee you that will get in the way of you making thousands of dollars in the sales game. Don't bend over to pick up a penny and leave the quarters on the table.

DON"T MAKE MONEY YOUR PRIME OBJECTIVE! BE THE BEST AND THE MONEY WILL ALWAYS BE THERE!

This is not to say that you don't keep your eyes open, listen to offers and generally know what the market is for a winner like you. That's just good business. Plus we all need a safety net in case some jerk becomes our boss or worse yet, takes over the company. You'd be surprised how great you feel when you

know that if anything happened, you would be looking for a job at most for an hour or two! That's real security!

Remember, you are part of the 20%. Most companies have at the most two people who fit in this mold and likely have just one, you. So if some pencil pushing fool is going to lose you over mere pennies then his loss is someone else's gain.

Remember, revenge is a very strong motivating factor. If someone in sales belongs to the exclusive 20% club and is hell bent on revenge, watch out! There is going to be a ton of business written and this sales person will stay out with a coal miners light cap on to prove that the other company made a huge mistake. And you know what? It never goes away! What a great motivational tool provided by of all things, your former employer. We all should taste the waters of this intoxicating beverage. <u>Revenge</u> is as good as it gets!! We should all consume this for breakfast (of course the breakfast of sales champions).

And you know what? The good companies they all know this, they aren't idiots, and would love to get their hands on you. So remember, money will never buy you security. Being at or near the top of your field will. No question about it! Case closed, let's move on.

CHAPTER SIX - ORGANIZED FOR SUCCESS

This is a real hard one for me to discuss. Why? Well, because first and foremost, I really am not that organized. Some people just love things perfectly arranged. They have to use a sharpened number 2 pencil to balance their checkbook and their desks are basically shrines to neatness. It seems like they are the most organized people on the face of this earth. Usually the best among sales professionals have trouble being organized. They live a helter skelter life, rushing from one account to another, always in a hurry, always accomplishing plenty...Does that describe you? It describes me and having been this way for quite a few years I have to stress the importance of being organized and what a difference it has made in my life as well as my career.

Begin by starting out your sales week by carefully writing down all the calls you need to make during that week. I usually do this over morning coffee when ambitions run high. What seems like a daunting task doesn't look quite so bad when it is put to paper. I use an envelope, write on the outside of it my calls, and then if I get any new cards or information I put them inside the envelope. At the end of the week when every call is crossed out with a see-thru marker I file it in a file box. This way I always have a record of what calls I have made for the week. I have a safe place to keep the new cards that I collect, and most importantly, even if my sales that period were not up to par (which has never happened), I can take encouragement from the fact that I completed every call on my agenda. For me, I can't feel good about my week or myself if all the calls don't get crossed out. Never cross one out or off if you don't do it. Save it for the next time. When you finally line it out you will get a real sense of accomplishment! I can look back years now and see the calls I made, the new cards I collected and feel very, very successful. Another suggestion is to put ten of your business cards in your pocket. The trick is that you have to hand them out before you quit. This one works every time.

ALWAYS WRITE UP A LIST OF CALLS! COMPLETE IT AND SELF-ESTEEM WILL FOLLOW YOU EVERYWHERE!

Now if anyone has the audacity to doubt your work ethic, all you have to do is bring in your file box and show them step by step, week by week what you have been doing. After their eyes go back in their sockets, I am sure they will leave you alone for awhile, knowing you are working as hard as you can.

This is a nice time to bring up the point that we all have to work with our superiors. And really, all of us have to work with one another. If you're the best, they like to ride with you, get pointers from you and if your performance is lacking they want to encourage you. At least that's what they say! Believe me, most of the time they want to make sure you are working. Plain and simple!

If anyone works with you, give them the sales day of their life! Start early, take no breaks, skip lunch, bring a snack for yourself (for energy), and stay out late. Hustle all day long breaking a sweat if necessary. If you do this I guarantee that your riders will

become less and less frequent.

Most managers want to go out for a couple of hours, make a few calls, and get back to their jobs. Don't let them! Make them pay for working with you. Next time when they think of bothering someone, they certainly won't pick on you. Why? Because you worked the pants off them! Remember, if they are a manager, they certainly aren't used to making lots of sales calls. And you know for a certainty that they have never skipped lunch in their life. So show them what being a salesman is all about. Show them that being out in the field is a little more work than they bargained for.

Of course, for me personally, I am one who doesn't like to stop for lunch. Lunch is a momentum loser. If you have built up any momentum throughout the day, you lose it at lunchtime. Then you have to start up all over again after the break and sometimes salespeople just can't re-stoke their competitive juices. Unfortunately, their sales day is now over and there's nothing more they can accomplish except to go home. Now you know why if it's up to me I skip lunch!! I bring a high fiber energy bar or sometimes I'll get a cup of coffee or sometimes maybe I'll have a tuna sandwich with me, but lunch is definitely a no-no. Lunch is not for champions. Wow, look at all the restaurants who hate me now! Don't worry, I'll live. (Plus, look at all the money you save!)

One time I worked with one of the owner's of my company since he expressed an interest in riding with me. Great, I said, I start early and don't stop until it gets too dark to see. Now this owner was also a friend of mine so I really didn't have too much to prove and I do work very hard! So, I drove to the outer limits of my territory which was a good hour away from the office and started bagging some business. To be fair though, it's nice sometimes to have someone like my owner friend who had some talent and knew when to shut up and when to talk. That will always help you. Some customers that might not have ordered do so. Why? Because if you called on them a few times they don't want you to look bad in front of the big cheese.

But unfortunately, most sales managers are nerds. They are sales people who couldn't make it in the field. So it's those kind that you want to absolutely get off your back. I tell you, one ten-hour day with no breaks for anything and they'll never want to kill themselves again. Guaranteed! Now getting back to my boss, we worked for a good five hours and he was practically begging me to have lunch. I drove through Taco Bell for him and continued to work. About the time that most would feel they had done enough, I had a double espresso and drove clear to the other side of my territory again, a good 35 minutes in the other direction from the office and his car. Once the coffee was having a positive effect, I made numerous calls when I knew he was exhausted. But I didn't stop yet. I had him where I wanted him. I continued to work and work and work! Finally dusk came. I drove towards the office and I could see a huge sigh of relief was expounded by Mr. Big. His eyes were bulging, his feet were sore and he was done! But I wasn't! Now after dark I picked up a few calls that always worked later or who had paged me that day. I was tired too, but I wanted my work day to be remembered. Finally at about 8 p.m. we pulled into our office compound. I asked him if he wanted to help me with the paper work that I perform on a daily basis, and he quickly excused himself. Enough was enough!!

Now I ask him to go with me and before he responds you can see his minds eye go back to that hellacious day and he always makes up an excuse. In his opinion every day compares to that day for me. No wonder, he reasons, I'm the top salesman! I work my butt off and that's obviously what you do and want them to think.

Remember, we're dealing with a product that stinks and you certainly don't want some sales wanna-be tailing you and messing up your aura. What are people going to think when they see a nerd and he's your boss? This is not good. Spend as little time with this kind of manager that you can and you'll benefit immeasurably from it.

Another way to be organized is to have a nice clean desk and car. It only takes five maybe ten minutes a week to arrange your things. Do it! Not only will others think more of you but you'll definitely feel better about yourself too. There's nothing worse than working around or in a mess all day. Again it takes such a short time to do it none of us have an excuse that is even worthy of being considered.

BE NEAT AND ORGANIZED - IT PAYS!!

Your personal appearance is also very, very important! Your product stinks but you shouldn't. It's extremely imperative that you dress for success. Be as classy as your budget allows you. Buy the most expensive clothes and have them pressed and laundered professionally and you will have a distinct advantage over everyone. I'd rather see someone have two changes of clothes that are super nice and elegant than a closet full of ordinary normal attire. We need to set ourselves apart from our competition. If you drive up to a client in a nice car (hopefully a Lexus or a Mercedes Benz), have expensive, professionally pressed clothes, and tasteful jewelry accenting your clothes and look like a million bucks you'll always fare much better than the one who makes their calls in a beater car, with wrinkled cheap clothes.

However, expensive clothes and pressing costs money. Most can't afford it! That's true, but in your line of work you can't afford not to look the part.

Speculate to accumulate! In other words, in our game you have to spend money to make it! Come on you cheapskates, in any business you enter usually there's an investment that needs to be made. When I went into carpet cleaning I had to buy a van, a cleaning machine (very expensive), many uniforms, invoices, telephone answering machine and much, much more! In sales you just strap it on and go! What an advantage we have! So calm down and go out and buy yourself some super nice clothes. Invest in a flashy automobile and always be clean cut and without a wrinkle. Do this and people won't notice your product stinking up the joint! But answer me this, if you've convinced your clients that you are the best salesperson in the world and you don't look the part, do you think they are going to believe you? No way. Now if you put out the whole package and don't miss a trick, there is absolutely no reason why your customers won't perceive you as you want and need to be seen. Dress for success, there's no other way period!!

Last paragraph I threw out one of those fancy sales terms that we all play ping-pong with.<u>Speculate to accumulate!</u> Never is this term more true than when you are hawking a lousy product. If it takes cutting your commission to make a sale, do it. Speculate to accumulate! If it takes treating everyone to pizza, do it. Speculate to accumulate! If the man who gives you orders likes steak, buy him a side of beef. Speculate to accumulate! If your customer likes professional sports go out and buy him the best tickets that money will buy. Again, speculate to accumulate! This is an edge that you can buy. If we figure in the WIIFM theory (What's In It For Me), face it, when it comes time to cut the budget or evoke changes, make it as hard as possible for them to skip you. Make yourself an attractive package that not only makes them money but also takes care of entertainment, food and other thoughtful, fun activities. "Boy, I don't want to throw Mike out. I love those Giants tickets." Believe me, if a customer loves you he will find a way to love your product.

But this is sometimes a very expensive proposition you say. I don't make enough to foster these types of bills! Wrong, genius, you'll never be able to afford any nice things in life if you don't speculate to accumulate.

I'll give you an example. One of my customers is a Saturn dealer. All Saturns look alike and basically sell themselves. If someone is interested in buying a Saturn, usually they will look it up in the Yellow pages and find them on their own. But my client was interviewing all the ad people to see who he was going to throw some money at. During our first conversation, I told him that if he did ads with me I would include him in my family of clients. This privilege would enable him to go to any event, at any time, with prime seats. You see, since I'm the best and have been around for years, I also have a ton of contacts imagined or real. Now immediately he said he was a huge fan of the Chicago Bulls and that they would be in town next week. The only problem was that the game was sold out for almost a year! I promised him tickets. He said if I delivered, not only would I get an ad but all his business. Music to my ears! I made a lot of calls, pulled some strings and for 600 bucks got him two courtside seats. 600 bucks you say! Wow! But think about it. He had a wonderful time, had great seats and I even found a way to pay for his beer and hot dogs. Now since he had such a wonderful time, I became wonderful, my product was seen as the best, and he's been with me for two and a half years now. All told I've made at least $6,000 from that account, and you must admit I certainly speculated to accumulate. I put out $600 to make $6,000, Not bad, huh. With that type of return maybe I should go into the stock market. Or better yet, perhaps I should just stick to what I do best, selling and winning.

Also don't forget to keep your expenses in this regard. It's a wonderful tax deduction. That's hard to believe isn't it, even Uncle Sam helps you to be a hero. Use everything to your advantage and remember I talked about your nice clothes and keeping them pressed and a car to look good. Don't look now but I also believe these are tax deductions also. Check with your accountant though, I'm not qualified to give advice in this area but I am qualified to tell you to take advantage of all the breaks you can get.

Remember you need all the help you can garner. Why? Because, Soupy Sales, you are selling a product that isn't as good as the others. So my sales brethren, in conclusion, spare no expense in looking good and pleasing your customer. It's like that rubber beach ball that you push down in the pool. It always comes up twice as hard as you pushed it down. Be the best and you'll have lots of people thanking you for making their life just a little bit better! What a privilege, what an opportunity. Don't be cheap. Be the best! It's really quite simple, isn't it? Speculate to accumulate!

SPECULATE TO ACCUMULATE! IT PAYS LARGE SALES DIVIDENDS!

CHAPTER SEVEN - SALESPERSON - NO, CONSULTANT - YES

I remember one older guy who was a very interesting sales guy. He used to tell his customers "I'm not a salesman, I'm a serviceman. I've come here to give you good service." That's a good one, huh? Yes indeed! But what I want to do is take that idea, not being a salesman, and improve upon the premise. We obviously don't want our clients to view us as just sales people period! If they do, you'll never get anywhere with them. Don't forget we are trying very hard to sell a shoddy product, so if you get caught trying to sell someone on it you'll lose them for life. This is where consultant selling comes in. Become an expert in your particular field!!

I was in the car business so I subscribed to every morning newspaper in the area and before I left for the day I'd scan the pages to see which of my customers were using this medium. When I saw them (hopefully that day) I always asked them "How's your ad in the newspaper doing? It looked like a great ad." Now I'm in the catbird's seat because first of all I've shocked them by paying such close attention to their business and by drawing attention to the ad. I'm the first one who is going to hear of its success or failure. I even go so far as to report mistakes or bad placements in competing publications. Why? Because I care about my account. They always appreciate it because I'm truly showing them that I'm on their team. I want them to sell their product. We are partners. If the ad works I praise their decision and

suggest slight modifications to make it an even better ad. If it doesn't I never put down their decision, but give suggestions on what kind of buyers pick up that paper, what the demographics are and finally what has worked in that type of medium in the past.

I'll give you an example. One of my best accounts was having an off month and decided he'd put about 30 spot ads in the local newspaper. I saw them and remarked to him that I wished him success. When it didn't work too well he told me and said he'd had it and was never going to use them again. This should have been music to most ears but I, Mr. Consultant, took it a step further and explained that the newspaper's circulation was primarily in the ritzy, well-to-do area of town. These people are traditionally interested in high line cars like Acura Legends or Mercedes Benz's. Certainly the newspaper was no place to try and sell older, lower priced vehicles. And that's unfortunately what he was trying to do. He was milking a cow that had no milk. He did have two cars that fit the newspaper's criteria and demographic pattern so I told him to try those. He did and when he sold one I became his guru of sales. From that time forward I used to get calls from him telling me he just bought such-and-such car and he would always ask where he should advertise it, I was always happy to help him and in so doing solidified myself forever in that dealership. Pretty good, huh?

It's important friends, the more information you can find out about your particular field, the better consultative salesperson you're going to be. Get the sales trade magazines your customers get. Go to Saturday grand openings with the family. Immerse yourself in your particular business and the rewards will be handsome. Some might disagree though. "That's a lot of work and a lot of reading. I'm usually too tired for that." You know what my response is? Let me ask you an important question. Are you too tired to cash big fat whopping checks? Or will you be more tired looking for a new job? Guess I said a mouthful, huh? Stand out!! Get up an hour early to plan your day and read everything you can get your hands on. After a good breakfast (which I absolutely believe in) and maybe some juice or coffee, sit down and read. It's a great time, you're all alone, everything's quiet, you're fresh and what you can get done in 15 minutes would take you an hour any other time of the day.

Again, become the expert in your field! <u>Have the ability to suggest things to your customer that don't always benefit you.</u> Once you do this you will gain their trust and respect. If you do it right they will consult you before any move or decision they make. I can't tell you the amount of times I've had customers ask me about another medium, my competition or even what's going on in the field! I always give my little report about what's selling, what's not and who is having the most success. If you correctly dive into your field and know inside and out all the nuts and bolts, you'll greatly enhance your value to your customer.

In the car business certain cars are dogs and others are hot. A Cadillac before a certain year has a T4100 engine in it that blows up regularly, So if one of my customers buys one of these I share my knowledge with him. If he already knew about this glitch he'll at least decipher that I know my business and if he wasn't aware of this it will affect the price he puts on it and the type of activity he will expect. Know your stuff! Customers always open up to me because they know that I'm interested in their success. If they sell lots of product and make tons of money, I'm happy period! And believe me, if things are going well, people usually don't change them!

Always remain in control but absolutely don't send one of your clients to someone else and lose touch. Follow up so you can keep your hooks in them. It's o.k. to tell a prospect about a competitor who might be able to provide a service for them that you can't, but control it by making contact with that company and arranging for a solution to their problem. One way you keep a customer happy and your property, the other way you might be opening yourself up to losing your prospect to another shark like yourself. You make the moves for your customer and then you'll be the hero who saved the day and, more importantly, since you're the expert why should your client need the services of anyone else?

BE A CONSULTANT, NOT A SALESPERSON, AND REAP THE REWARDS.

CHAPTER EIGHT - KNOW YOUR COMPETITION

It may seem very obvious to all concerned but you'd be surprised how many in the sales game put their heads in the proverbial sand when it comes to knowing their competition. Your competition is exactly that! They are competing for the same dollars you are, Bubba!! Remember, the pie is only so big. Therefore you have to be extremely aware of those who are trying to get in your pocket. And that's exactly what they're trying to do! Don't fool yourself. I don't know what makes a salesperson happiest, bagging a new account or stealing one from somewhere else. Now to protect yourself against sales piracy and to pirate customers away from others you have to know your competition! I'll say that one more time since it's so important.

KNOW YOUR COMPETITION!!

It does you absolutely no good to be hawking a product that gets no one's serious attention because you're overpriced, not a fit, not needed or been talked so bad about for so long that you're basically "untrusted". To break down these barriers know what the other companies are doing. C'mon now, you can do it!

I personally like to scoop them on their own specials. Look at the power you have in your market if you can tell each one of your clients what the salesmen from the other companies are coming up with next. At this point you're in a position to advise them on whether it's really a special or not, if a better deal can be had, or if it's a disguised effort to exhume more money from your client's pockets. If the offer is a genuine one, be prepared to match it, or even better yet, beat it. Imagine the chagrin on your competitor's face when he goes to all his calls all charged up and ready to sell and you've beaten him to the punch! Wow, now that's a thrill! The only way to get this kind of information is to know your competition inside and out! What are the times of year when they have specials? Ask a customer of yours to phone and ask! What are their strengths, and more importantly what are their weaknesses? I like to point out both sides of the picture. At every call I mention my competition favorably and point out where their strengths lie and of course where these can't hold a candle to me. Remember gang, our product is probably not as good as the other guys, so we have to know every move our competition is going to make. Memorize their prices. Know their rep's schedules. Sometimes it's to your advantage to be at a call at the same time as they are because the order taker doesn't want to be bothered twice. Other times he wants everything dealt with individually. In this case <u>always get to your customer first!</u> Don't let him or her tell you that they've already spent their budget with the competition. That's your fault. Get to know everyone's schedule, and just in case someone knows yours, change it up. Don't be predictable.

I had a guy whose prime objective in his existence was to make my life miserable. He got my schedule down pretty good and decided he was going to call on my accounts before I did. He got to two prospects and fortunately for me I got a call from one of them. I always mention that lunch is on me if any news from the territory is thrown my way. A nice lunch

too! And sure enough, my competition was working on Sunday! What a drag! I got on my work clothes and went out in the field. At each call I told them that business was so bad for the other guys that now they were working Sundays. Certainly since their business is off you wouldn't want to get too heavily involved with them now would you?

It worked. Instead of my competitor getting new business and a pat on the back for working Sunday, they looked at him with suspicious eyes. However, on the other hand I've worked Sundays or an unusual day and it's always been a wonderful day for me! Always dress casually! In the morning, as a rule, the client is much more relaxed and since it's not a day that they're used to seeing you and you're dressed properly, it's more of a social call than a business call! When you can catch your prospect at a time like this, wonderful things can happen.

That's why it is <u>so</u> very important to make any social events that occur within your industry. Get to know your people on another level and it can only benefit you! The respect and familiarity you will engender will always make it worth your time and energy.

One thing you need to be careful about is to never overstay your welcome! Spend just enough time for everyone to see you and have a brief conversation. Rub shoulders with the people you need to see and leave. Don't hang out and have a few cocktails. Keep yourself above those situations. Be a class act and you'll start to cash classy checks. What a nice fit for the case of being a consultant rather than a salesper-

son. A consultant knows the other guys prices, the area they cover, their strengths and weaknesses. A salesman only knows his products, its features and benefits and not much else. Now, I'm not telling you not to be an expert on your line, you have to be! I'm saying to take it a step further! We all know the features and benefits of our stuff add nauseum. Now know the other guys too and you'll be a real force in your industry. I guarantee it. If you become a consultant salesperson, soon you'll have to consult an accountant for the tax breaks you'll desperately need because of those big meaty large paychecks. That sounds appetizing, doesn't it? It had better.

CHAPTER NINE - LISTEN, STUPID!!

Sometimes we in the sales field fall in love with something that's strictly off limits. It's a very attractive, absolutely tempting love. Something we've probably had a hankering for most of our adult life. It seems there's no better sound and everything that comes from it, believe it or not, is either hysterically funny or perceptionally right.

Now before you get too excited I'd better stop and name this wonderful love of your life. Yes, it's your own voice. C'mon, be honest, we all like hearing ourselves talk. Our voice is one of the most favorite of all the objects we call our own. Think of all the wonderful things it does for each and every one of us. It can propose to your love, tell stories to your children, order food at a restaurant. It can make people laugh, it can express deep appreciation, it can make friends, it can make someone's day. What a powerful tool, huh? Harness it now! As much good as this little jewel (the tongue) can perform for you, it can and will get you in trouble.

I stress that each of us likes the sound of our own voice. We rely on it for so much. So when we get into trouble or are involved in a stressful situation we tend to rely on "talking" to solve our problems or to gain an advantage. Be different - listen! Yes, oh sales wannabe's, listen. That's a six letter word that can spell success faster than any other word in the English language. If you truly listen, and that's not just taking a breath between statements, you'll be one of the best.

Look at your prospect and concentrate on what he or she is saying. Taking notes is a great idea if you can pull it off! You might say, "Since you're so important to me do you mind if I take notes so that I can have your every need on paper? It will make it much easier and efficient if I write down everything!" After you've listened and perceived the clients needs, <u>always count to ten</u>. Really do this!! It allows your prospect to come up with more information and remember, information is your ally and waiting also gives respect to what was just said. In the theater or the movies there's always a pause either before or after something important. By pausing, you're attaching importance to what was just said. It may seem like an eternity to you but believe me it will be raining pennies from heaven if you follow this simple but effective tool.

Practice listening in every facet of your life. It will help you to develop into a sales machine! None of us can take Sales 101 in school can we? So we have to practice in real life. Listen twice as much as you talk!! That's why we have <u>two ears and only one mouth</u>! If you listen to someone well, with concentration you'll be able to decipher what they really want. Do it in your life and of course it will come out naturally in the field. And here's a little bonus you thought you'd never get from this book - your relationships in life will be better. Maybe I should go into psychiatry too - No chance! (But I wonder?)

LEARN THE ART OF LISTENING - SHUT UP!

CHAPTER TEN - WHAT ABOUT HOME?

C'mon now, you're wondering what the heck this one is all about, aren't you? There's two ways to look at the question. One, the usual jazz about how important your family is to your success. No genius at work here. If a salesperson is having trouble at home it usually carries over into the workplace. Ours is an emotional game and if your emotions are being spent on anything but your job my friend, you are at a distinct disadvantage. Since none of us have perfect home lives you have to find a way to leave your problems where they originated. I look at my job as an escape where I can hide from all the things that might plague me at home. Look at it that way and you'll relax and definitely benefit immeasurably. If you're like me, most of your friends are your customers (or at least they should be) so where else can you drive around, visit with friends, tell jokes, write a few legible sentences and get paid handsomely? The White House? No, wrong - this is no place for political jokes even though that one's not too bad. Sales is where it's at! That's why it's a privilege that we all earn and respect! So your home life is important but if it's messed up more then it's right, learn to use your job as an escape. Wow, what a job.

But there's another facet to the question what about home? Now let's pursue that area. Why? Because it's important to those of us who have a product that stinks; as well as those fortunate souls that sell a winner. (That has a nice ring to it, huh?) Home is where we store all our accumulated posses-

What About Home?

sions. One of the most important things that we put on our side of the ledger is our existing customer base. Yes, these are the ones who always order. A trained monkey could take care of them, so the sales guru in the sky has thrown you a gimme. That's nice because with all the hard work one has to do to get new accounts and keep them, especially when they're difficult, all of us could use as many of these as possible! However, one interesting area that is seldom mined and should be, is either selling more to your existing clients or asking them for referrals. Obviously whatever you're doing with them, they like. Why not go for more? Yes, there's a little risk involved but I tell you it'll pay off tremendously.

It's at this point that I have to relate a super sales story told by Earl Nightingale of Nightingale Conant. It's his saga gang, so all the credit should go to him for running this one down. (I'll tell the story by memory, that way the important lessons will come from my heart.)

As the epoch goes, an African farmer was very intent on owning a piece of the African dream, a parcel of land. He worked hard and saved and worked some more until he was able to procure the land. Most of us buy land so we can live on it but this gentleman wanted his land to make him happy and rich. It seems that farming was harder than he expected and the payoffs were slim compared to the amount of effort that was expended. At this particular time an acquaintance of his came down from the Congo or some other mountainous region and had found a sizable amount of diamonds. The diamond bug bit him and the man unsatisfied with his lot in life (no pun

intended) sold everything to chase down his fortune in the mines. Several years later however, exhausted and humbled, the penniless farmer hurled himself from a high place to his death. What a shame this had to happen! Why?

Because unknown to him, the person who bought his land one day was fishing the river that circumnavigated his property. Something shiny caught his eye. He picked up this rather large rock, saw that it was huge and shiny and also was very interesting, so he put it on his mantle as a conversation piece. A visit from a neighbor produced a very interesting response. On seeing this huge chunk of a diamond, the neighbor fainted. When he recovered, he said he'd never seen a diamond as large as this one in his life! The farmer responded that it couldn't be a diamond and certainly wouldn't be valuable because there were so many chunks just like that one in the river.

Yes it seems that the river was fed by one of the biggest diamond mines ever discovered on any continent including Africa. This man, who bought the property from the original farmer who wanted to find his fortune in diamonds was rich beyond belief. What a story, huh?

The lesson is a very valuable one and one I've never forgotten. All the first farmer had to do was look at what he owned and he would have found all he was looking for. There were acres of diamonds (the name of the story) right beneath his feet. How many acres of diamonds do we step over?

When we visit an existing client who's happy we should take the time and pursue all angles from his perspective. Why go bouncing here and there when our best chance is right beneath our feet? Every time it becomes too easy to handle an account look for ways to expand. Remember if something doesn't grow it's either dead or sick and we never want this to happen to us. So dear ones, be thankful for those advocates but give more than thanks for what they give you. Work them and see if there truly are acres of diamonds just waiting to be mined. Don't trip over the treasure in your territory. It's right there at your best customer's doorstep.

P.S. - Thanks to Earl Nightingale for a true story that touched my life!!

CHAPTER ELEVEN - EARLY BIRD, CATCH THAT WORM!

Congratulations sales scholar. You've finished ten whole chapters. So, c'mon now, keep reading. This pain is kind of like eating peas when you were a kid. They tasted horrible but they were good for you! So with this in mind remember that this may be an unpopular chapter, but it's one that absolutely has to be discussed. Yes, I know most salespeople don't even own an alarm clock. We've earned that right. It's one of the perks of continually taking a chance with your paycheck each month. But if you're one who sleeps in, lose the habit quickly! I don't care if you're a nighthawk or if you need lots of sleep. It's a fact that those who use their alarm clock and get up early definitely have an advantage over all! Do it! Set your alarm early and get up! That's right, lazy bones, make your coffee, have your breakfast and be ready for work at least <u>one to two hours</u> earlier than you normally would start. Why? It's very simple. If you start early and have your momentum and energy (a salesperson's best friend), ready to go when you hit that first call, you're absolutely ready to conquer!! Imagine what happens when the prospect drags himself into work and you are the first one he sees! Now you've got it! That's an unfair advantage, huh? Always get them coffee, and as soon as it starts to kick in, assertively grab their business. Everyone likes to start his or her day off and running so you can be the impetus for them achieving that goal.

In my 25 years experience, decision makers are always at the office early. If you need to start your day on the phone, that's o.k., just make sure you begin an hour or two earlier to take advantage of this phenomenon. Now, you still think sleep is more important than making those calls a little earlier? You lazy bag of bones! Let me explain, not only do you always catch the person in charge, but you always get your day off to a very positive start! You've achieved something, when most in your profession are still showering. This day goes better because you're building on a successful base and you ultimately feel much better about yourself. The early bird definitely catches the worm!! Start early and then if you're done a little early it's a nice reward.

When do you think you have the best chance of bagging an account? In the afternoon when they're probably not even there? Or if they are around, they've just had lunch and all they're thinking about is going home, as their food is digesting and making them sleepy? At this point in the day they are struggling just to make the last couple of hours and their mood certainly belies this factor. Now turn the tables, you are their first call in the morning, when perspectives are fresh and ambitions are in high gear. The coffee is just starting to take affect and this particular decision maker wants to get something done. He wants to start this day off with a bang!! And here you come! Wait, stop, that's an unfair advantage. Where are the other salespeople? Too bad!. You got up, you earned it and with a product that doesn't exactly tip the scales, you need all the advantage you can get. Take this piece of advice and excel - lead the pack! The early bird always catches the worm, but remember he has to be up and flying around to catch that first worm! I've never seen a worm drop into a nest and you'll never ever achieve success by rolling over in bed and turning off that alarm! Get up and out and win!!

We have discussed it in previous chapters that sales is an emotional game and one way I find to help myself through the valleys along with the peaks is to always start and finish my day with a strong, supportive client. For years I've driven out of my way to start with someone who appreciated me and always ordered! My sales psyche was always built up and it seemed like I didn't have some of the problems others had to deal with. Hold on, I'm not finished! I also ended my day with a strong supportive account so that I could take that successful feeling home with me. There's no greater torture for you or your family than to take home a bad day. So end it well, and it will give you a reason for starting early the next day. Most importantly, it will help you forget your work while you're with your family. When you're with the wife and kids or husband or boyfriend or whatever, be with them! Don't take work home with you. We all need time to rejuvenate, to get away and get ready for the next day. Tomorrow will come quick enough, walk away from work and watch out for that telephone. It's an enemy! It can rob you of more time than any bandit around. Talk with your sales buddies about work at work, not at home! If you have a pager, bury it in a drawer until the morning. Whatever it was that someone wanted, it will keep until tomorrow. It's important to take time to smell the roses, appreciate what you've got and lick your wounds. Blow out your ballasts so that the next time you run you'll be free of any lingering doubts or activities from the day before. This is very important and will

Early Bird, Catch That Worm!

keep you on the job and in the front lines for years, after everyone else is burnt out! And while we're on the subject, always take your vacation! Some regrettably like to take the money. Others don't trust anyone with their clients. But it's a nice chance for the person (including management) who is courting your accounts to see how hard you work during the week! If you're lucky you can even move forward a little while you're basking in the sun somewhere. And then when you get back, guess what? You'll have brand new adventures for your customers to listen to. You need vacation! Period! You need personal time! Period! Take it or you won't be long for this business. If you don't, you'll undoubtedly suffer from stress or burnout and that's no fun! Plus, c'mon, we are only on the earth for a short time - don't spend it all working. Save time for your family, recharge your batteries and you'll be a much more effective salesperson. Believe me!

CHAPTER TWELVE - YOU'RE ON THE INSIDE!

Sounds like you've been arrested, huh? I probably should be thrown in jail for being as successful as I've been. But here we're going to develop the concept of working at your customers place of business as one of his employees. Some are up front about what they need to accomplish by doing this, others go in the back door, take a job find out what it's like to be in their prospects shoes and move on without telling anyone. I say be honest. Tell your client you want to spend a few days working for him, observing what goes on so you, the super salesperson, can better serve his needs. Milk this one! Tell me, how many in this sales game would give up a weekend or a couple of days off to experience what their clients are going through? Not many! But when you break it down into percentages you'd probably be safe to say that 20% of the sales force writes 80% of the business.Now you know why. The 20% sales force will stop at virtually nothing to serve or impress his client. I'll give you an example!

An account of mine was relocating to a brand new facility. They had gone from automatics to sporadic customers. I suggested, or they suggested I forgot, that we do a grand opening.This was my chance to shine! I handled most of the details, from spotlights to advertisement to radio coverage, newspapers and most importantly, entertainment. On the day of the event a clown appeared from nowhere handing out special treats (M&M's) to the kids. The manager knew who it was, but the rest of the working crew had no idea it was me! I spent $40 on the costume, bought a $10 wig and had my wife apply the makeup. I worked the event for a good five hours generally making everyone's day just a little better. On a side note that has nothing to do with our topic, <u>I really appreciate clowns now!</u> You know, they have a very weighty responsibility. Kids from all over came to shake my hand! Some were shy and had to be handled a certain way and others were bold wanting to see if my nose was real. (Yes, that's right, by pulling it! Ouch! It's mine!) But by and large, each child that day was positively affected by the clown. If this guy was grumpy or nervous or just unclown-like, a child's view of clowns would have been altered forever. So those of you who decide to go this route do so, but by all means remember when you put on the garb of a clown do so with respect and reverence for their position in a little child's eyes. There is nothing like the twinkle in a little ones eyes when they see a clown. Make them laugh! Make them happy or don't be a clown.

Anyway, where was I? That's right, I spent five hours making everyone laugh! It was exhilarating! Soon everyone knew it was me. The rumor spread like wildfire and now the owner of the company who I had never had the privilege to meet, came up to see me with a refreshing, cooling, strong cocktail. I made it! Salesman's heaven! Much appreciation was shown to myself and my company and the word even got out to my competition. Now when the other salespeople call or make contact at other accounts, they'd ask, "Was the clown by yet?" or "What's the clown doing?". Of course in their little demented sales minds they think they're insulting me, but every reference to my day as a clown is a supreme compliment

to my industriousness. This guy will stop at nothing to help and please his customers. Imagine that! However, there is one downside to doing something like that! Unfortunately whenever anyone has a grand opening or some sort of event they remember the clown and want him to appear. What do you say? Remember, before you answer you're swimming in water that's polluted, use every tool you can to stay afloat. Do more, not less, and you'll be rewarded handsomely. Dust off that clown suit and go for it! Stop clowning around and blow the horn of success. It takes so little.

The whole day I spent at this event also allowed me a backstage look at what my clients were going through. By walking their walk, not only was I one of them, but I could empathize with their particular situation. Do it! Sit behind your client's desk and see things from his or her perspective daily. They always try to solve a plethora of problems by using virtually the same solutions. Show them new ones! From a different perspective you can see things they can't! <u>Help, help, help and you'll sell, sell, sell!</u> I can't overemphasize how important it is to see things from your clients perspective! If you do, you've done your homework and you'll stand in a place that few sales people stand. Ask questions, (to yourself) what would I do if I were running their show? How could they save money? When you have the answers share them <u>one at a time</u> with your order giver. Make him look like a hero and a genius and he'll never forget you. Remember we never want to make ourselves look good! We want to make our decision maker look good. Our job is to cash the big checks, not garner a fabulous resume. Feed your family, not your ego and you'll always have a place in everyone's budget!

What was that I just said, something about feeding your family, not your ego? That sounds like a wonderful subject for our next chapter. Turn the page and read on. We're really making great progress here!

CHAPTER THIRTEEN - FEED YOUR FAMILY, NOT YOUR EGO!

We've all heard this one, it's nothing new! But for those of us who have a product that's lacking something, these are words to live by! To translate into terms you can understand better, massage your checkbook with big entries, make deposits in your bank account and not in your already bulging ego. Remember a few chapters back when we discussed being the best? It seems like this kind of contradicts that, doesn't it? But alas, sales compadres, it takes the best to put others before yourself.

DON'T TAKE CREDIT FOR ANYTHING

Give it all to the guy who writes the checks. Make him into a successful manager and you'll be a successful salesperson. Remember though, our product probably can't do that alone but our knowledge of his trade will. This is where knowing his business better than he does is so, so very important! Get every piece of information you can. Get all his trade magazines, scour the internet, read the fictitious name statements in the paper. Be an expert in your field of expertise. Be on the cusp of what's new. Immerse yourself daily, and like that beach ball that you push down in the swimming pool you'll be propelled to immeasurable heights. I know it's tough propping someone up who is not as smart as you are but that's life bubba! Chances are that this poor guy or gal has to work 60-70 hour weeks and is stuck at one location. It all evens out! You know you're the best. Your family knows you're wonderful, who else really counts?

There are virtually thousands of opportunities to swallow your pride. When you don't, no one wins, especially you! Let me give you an example.

I had a client who wasn't having much success with my product. He told me he was going to go a different direction, so I was trying to salvage something to keep my foot in the door, and his boss walked in. He asked me who I was, and I told him. He rudely told me that they had spent way too much money on things like mine and that they were no longer interested. At this point I had my man looking on with interest and the big boss staring me down. What was the super salesperson going to do? The line was drawn in the sand! Unfortunately, my ego got the best of me and I haughtily told him that others in his area were doing quite well with my services. What was he talking about, I queried? Well he told me that he had checked around and everyone who was using me had an off month and those not availing themselves of my services were doing very well. (Probably a lie). But now it was getting interesting. Tommy, my order giver, was looking on in astonishment that someone would stand up to his big boss. My ego was definitely getting bigger, kind of like a balloon! But now he pulled rank on me and said since he owned the company I had seen my last check. I one-upped him and I said since I was part owner of my company, a big shot just like he was, he was truly making a big mistake. Tommy was looking on with renewed faith in his little salesman. Wow, he was dealing with an owner and didn't even know it! But this big shot (me) walked out empty-handed, never to return. I blew it. When the big boss walked in, instead of exchanging banter with him I should have excused myself and humbly called back another time. <u>Never confront!!</u> Run away and live to fight another day. Since it was the first of the month the owner probably had just seen his bills for the previous 30 days. Since his business was off it was not money well spent, was it?. The timing was bad for my visit and I should have cut and run, or even better yet, I should have asked someone else a little lower on the totem pole how their previous month was. I would have then learned that it wasn't a good time, that upper management was on the warpath and if I wanted to keep my scalp, to retreat. But I didn't do that! And when I was challenged I fed my ego and not my family. Ouch, that hurts. Tommy, remember him, was dutifully impressed with me. But unfortunately because of my untimely discussion with the boss he told me he could never order from me again. He was very sorry and I still had him as a friend, I even had his respect, but ultimately I lost that account. When his boss got involved I should have agreed with everything he said. I should have expressed concern and understanding. If I was smart I should have said of course if I were in his shoes I would do the very same thing! That's a good decision, sir! This would leave the door open for future visits and would allow you to make another friend. It doesn't do the ego much good but it does help you to keep in focus what's really important! <u>The customer, dummy, not you!!</u> Always remember that! You're a second-class citizen, your customer is king. It's a privilege to be in the same room as your client not the other way around. Feed your ego and you'll lose every time. Let the other sales fools be proud. Stay humble and you'll gain favor and approval for your actions. He who laughs last, laughs best!

CHAPTER FOURTEEN - THANK YOU!

Magic words! Really. I'm serious! In our modern electronic society, fast moving, fast talking and fax machines have become the norm. But listen good on this one! Nothing, "absolutely nothing", takes the place of a firm handshake and a look straight into someone's eyes. This of course, takes effort, an effort that you as a salesperson have to be willing to expend. The more effort, the more results, especially in the "little things". Lots of little things add up to something very, very big! Success!! This one factor can separate you from the rest!

One of the best ways to begin is to pick up a sales book from the 1950's or 1960's. Dale Carnegie is probably one who you'll stumble across but there are many others. This will enable you to go back to the basics. One basic tenet that has served me very well are the two words that very few use effectively. Thank you! "Oh, come on, I always say thank you to my customers. I say it so much it's probably not even heard." You see, that's what I'm getting at. Thank someone with a card, a gift, some sort of expression that stands out! A thank you card is one of the most underrated tools of our trade! Thank everyone you know from your minister to your plumber. Those thank you's will always get you referrals. It's so rare for someone to actually take the time from their busy schedule to be thoughtful, that a thank you card or gift will always elicit a favorable response. Don't type it. Hand write your cards and you can either deliver them yourself or let the mail man do it! I think I like the postal service helping me out in this area because then you're not standing there like a panting dog waiting for your atta-boy. But occasionally personal service works out the best. It's funny how powerful these two words that are often neglected can be. They can be a big weapon in your sales arsenal. But like all tools if it is not used, it's without value!

Since we're getting old fashioned all of a sudden, don't forget about the other magic word - please! Yes I know as kids we were taught to say please until our wisdom teeth were finally implanted. But this word is very, very powerful. If you doubt its impact, think back to the last time someone said please to you. What did you do? At the very least it made you stop and think about your response. And you know what, when someone says please something in us wants to say yes. Try it, you won't believe the results. Obviously to be able to use the please word effectively you have to be familiar with your prospect. It might take a few unfruitful calls but believe me when you unleash the power of please you won't be disappointed. You'd be surprised how many salespeople (1) don't ask for an order and (2) don't say please! Incorporate asking and please in your sales arsenal and you'll be amazed at the results. To use please you have to be asking for something, so it's a good way to work this technique into your spiel. Who of us have stood at the door and turned away a girl scout selling cookies after she asked us? She doesn't even have to say please because all her emotions and actions cry it out! But don't forget, you have to set this one up, otherwise even those sheepdog eyes glistening with a tear won't get that yes you're looking for.

CHAPTER FIFTEEN - WALK IN BACKWARDS

Make things interesting for yourself! Change things up a bit every now and then by wearing something out of character for your personality. It could be simple. In my case I always wear a tie and look as good as I can, so for me it's wearing a polo shirt with some casual pants. Keep things alive and cooking by changing the day you call, the vehicle you drive, or your hairstyle. The importance of this can be demonstrated by a unique experience that I had. This one's original and I just have to share it with you.

For a good year I had been calling weekly on a rather old fashioned, by the book customer. He hated change and was a very tough sell. Imagine, a whole year with nothing to show for your efforts! Each time I visited, I tried to teach him something about my product, gave him some industry news or told a joke. But I just wasn't getting through!! In frustration I decided, what the heck, what do I have to lose. So, I saw him sitting at his rather large desk lost in thought. I walked through the door backwards and was rather uncoordinated and uncomfortable in doing so. He peered at me over his glasses and asked what in the world I was doing. I explained that since he'd never ordered anything from me in a year I might as well be pointed in the right direction when he gave me the old heave ho! He laughed and said sit down you rascal, you've earned my business. And you know what? He's been a very loyal advocate ever since! I dramatically changed the call didn't I? I got his attention and I guarantee you I wasn't bored walking in backwards to his office! And after all that time, I won! Shake things up, especially if it's not working, don't continue conducting business the same. Go in riding a horse if you have to. Be different. If you haven't gotten business in the traditional way, be unconventional.

Here's a good one that demonstrates what I'm talking about.

Victor Kiam of the Remington Blade Company was a young salesman working for I believe the Proctor & Gamble soap division. One day there were about 20-30 presentations of just about the same product and he was looking for an edge. So he went to the pet shop and purchased a monkey. He brought the animal with him to the sales presentation. Hidden under wraps was this monkey and when it was his turn he put the monkey on his back. The chimp jumped off his back onto an oval table that had about ten board of directors sitting around it. After knocking over several waters and messing up many assorted papers Kiam told an astonished group of buyers, "Let me get the monkey off your back. Buy Proctor & Gamble!" He got the monkey quickly and left amid a buzz of conversation. The next day in the field, everyone was talking about Victor and his unique pitch. Of course we all know that Victor Kiam went on to be a huge entrepreneur and if we use one tenth of his imagination and get 1/100 of his huge success we'll do real well. Hats off to a unique way of changing things up a bit and keeping it interesting. I'll leave the particulars of accomplishing this to you as you'll have to use your skill in adapting this valuable information to your particular situation. But above all, don't just think about it and chuckle. Do it! Dare to be different! Dare to succeed! Make your visit the highlight of an otherwise dull week and you'll reap the rewards.

Take it from me, not only do you keep yourself interested but your customers will love you for it and reward you.

CHAPTER SIXTEEN - DO IT NOW!

All of us have a tendency to procrastinate! As please and thank you are magic words to those of us in sales, procrastination is an ugly, gross word. It's a term that denotes absolutely nothing happening! If nothing happens, you don't get paid. It's as simple as that. Even if you're on a guarantee or a draw, face it if you do nothing that's exactly what you're going to end up with. The proverbial donut hole! Nothing. Don't put things off! Do it now! If you put it off until tomorrow, not only will tomorrow be more difficult, but you won't forget entirely about it until it's done. It's almost like a coward dying a thousand deaths. If you don't keep up with things you'll never amount to anything in the sales field. Early in the morning, early in the week, early in the quarter are words to live by. Start early and you probably won't get distracted in the late afternoon. Why? Because by the late hours of the day you'll have accomplished all you need to. And if it's your choice that you keep working, voluntary servitude works much better than slavery. It's much easier to keep a rock rolling down a hill after it's started. Beginning is the toughest! Con yourself, lie to yourself, reason anything to get into action. Once you're into the fray all sorts of wonderful things can happen! If it's your goal to call on five extra calls a day, get them in early. Then after accomplishing that and feeling darn good about yourself there's no telling what you can accomplish. Procrastination is a poison pill friend. Don't do it. It can eat away at your success and accomplishes nothing good! Not only will you feel rotten about yourself, but it's one bad habit that can not be hidden from others. If you're rushing around at the last minute trying to finish off your work because you've procrastinated, not only will you miss a whole lot of opportunities, but your work will be sloppy and probably wrong. When someone phones you or pages you, get right back to them! Not only will this pay off in increased revenue, but it will do wonders for your sales psyche as well. Doing it now also applies to a tough client or a tough problem. Remember the longer you put it off the bigger the problem gets! Don't procrastinate. See the guy that busts your chops early in the day, not later.

I remember one customer that definitely got under my skin. Since his business was closest to my home I always did him last. But you know what, the day was always ruined because I knew no matter what success I had during the day it was tempered by having to call on the customer from hell. So I rearranged my calls so I could do his call first and you'd be surprised how great my day was after he was taken care of! Even if he didn't order anything I was so relieved that he was out of the way that my day always got off to a roaring start. Play it smart. Don't let someone play you. If it's a case of diminishing returns, be selfish and take care of yourself on this one. If he says you have to call on him last, tell him you're too over scheduled at that time and that he'll have to pick an earlier time and day. Stand firm and he'll come around at least to working within your time frame. Protect yourself, remember you're all you've got. If the horse isn't running in the race he can't possibly win. So keep yourself on the track. Take care of yourself mentally as well as physically. Exercise, take walks, eat right and absolutely don't abuse yourself by overindulging in anything. Balance makes sense. Dollars and sense! If you have a thoroughbred racehorse you feed him the best hay and take good care of him. He's your meal ticket. Should you treat yourself any less better? You're the meal ticket and your family's racehorse. Stay on the track and I'll see you at the winner's circle!

CHAPTER SEVENTEEN - SALES MEETINGS, BANE OR BOOM?

Face it, sales meetings are a necessary evil. Do your best to be present at every single one! Listen, listen, listen. And when you're finished listening, listen again. Why do I say this? Because there's so much one can glean from a sales meeting. First of all, by listening to your sales associates you can observe the problems and challenges that are being faced daily in the field. Second, by listening at meetings you'll be able to incorporate any changes or price increases or specials immediately. Don't fight change! It's really a part of our playing field. By listening intently at sales meetings you'll be viewed as a cooperative employee, you'll learn what's important to your supervisors, and you'll ultimately benefit. If you are allowed to give a special deal or price by listening you'll be right on top of it. Don't show up late and daydream. These meetings are usually pretty short and can help you - really. Notice the operative word here is <u>"listen"</u>! Help where you can, but by no means ever dominate a meeting. This could cause stress between you and your immediate supervisor and believe me, any ideas or positive directions taken from a meeting will be credited to the one who ran it anyway! So shut up! Listen. Impress if you want to but here's another place where it's better to feed your family rather than your ego.

In all my years of attending these mandatory functions I've either been inspired to greater heights or been discouraged by someone whose job is hanging by a slender thread (the manager). Don't forget your product doesn't hold water, so since most don't apply themselves as well to the particular situation as you, cover your ears because managers get upset when they don't hit their numbers! Your manager as a last ditch effort will probably try every trick in the book to eke out any increase, meager or otherwise, from his or her troops. But Don't, and I repeat Don't, give away <u>any</u> of your hard earned secrets. It won't be appreciated, and you certainly won't be compensated for any of it. So pass the time constructively for <u>yourself</u> as best you can. Benefit from the meetings. Even if it just means a free breakfast and some coffee. Be thankful you don't have the same problems that others obviously have. Personally, I dig sales meetings. Most of my awards or benefits come at these. It's another way of inspiring the troops and nothing inspires me more than being recognized for my efforts. If you're fortunate enough to have a skilled manager, gain all you can from him or her. They are truly a rare, vanishing breed. If your superior is a goof, this doesn't give you an excuse to be one yourself. Maintain your professionalism and class and you'll always benefit from sales meetings. Consider a meeting like a fancy bulletin board. Gain information from them only, and don't feel you're wasting your time. They aren't and you're not! If you don't believe me, imagine no sales meetings. Sure you'd gain some time, but you'd never be in touch with others, never have any specials or deals, and you'd never be able to impress your superiors with anything other than your numbers. Wear your best outfits to these meetings. Use this opportunity to impress all who come into contact with you. In an era of networking you never know when you'll cash in on your expeditious

Sales Meetings: Bane or Boom?

handling of this sometimes sticky situation. And never use the meeting to air your dirty laundry. Never complain in front of anyone. It never comes across well and it's just not smart. If you need something, meet with your superiors one-on-one and express your needs. The chances of your problems being taken care of are much greater if you handle it this way, rather than throwing them out at a meeting for all to hear. Conduct yourself as a professional at all times, in all places, even in your rinky-dink sales meetings. Use everything to your advantage. Yes, even Sales Meetings!!

CHAPTER EIGHTEEN - MOTIVATE, MOTIVATE, MOTIVATE!

One way that I motivate myself is by setting goals. I know we've all had our fill of the old goal-setting talks. But my rub on this one is to tell everybody, even my sales associates, what my goals are! As cocky as I am sometimes, I even needle my brethren of the calls, talking as much stuff as possible. Wait a minute, you say, what happened to the guy who was supposed to be quiet? The dude with the feed your family, not your ego philosophy? Well here we turn the tables, and talk as much stuff as possible. Why? It's simple if you've got any pride, you don't want anyone on your sales team laughing at you. If you make a boast, live up to it. Since you're part of the 20% winning circle sometimes no one can challenge you. But here's where the fun comes in.

One time I took on a whole office of Salespeople. I told them that I was going to beat them single- handedly. That's right, oh astonished one. It was me (1) against seven! Imagine that! This accomplished a lot! As I said, there were seven people in that office and all of them took me seriously. A case of beer was on the line, and I'll tell you I never worked harder in my life than that week! My sales went up, and I made a whole lot more money than the case of beer cost. Also, because I had the guts to make that challenge, my superiors couldn't help but notice several things: one, that I was capable of doing the work of seven people; two, that I was leading by example; three, that they probably couldn't live without me and my numbers; and finally four, that I was the best! A lot was accomplished by my first, setting a goal and second, by telling and challenging everyone with it. Remember, when you put it out there on the line, there's no better motivation. Needless to say, there were no early days that week, and all my customers were of course in on the action. Again, I reinforced to them (my customers) as well as all who would listen how I was the golden one. I cashed a fairly large paycheck, was a hero to management, and even got a little respect from my associates.

You know there's all sorts of interesting little psych games you can play with yourself and others. But the important thing to remember is to tell everyone what's going on. Advertise, advertise, advertise! It's fun, and most importantly it pays! So gang, when you make a goal, that's great, but what's even better is when you advertise this goal to everyone and have to live up to your advance billing.

PRIVATE GOALS ARE GOOD, BUT ADVERTISED ONES ARE THE BEST...WHAT A MOTIVATION!!!

CHAPTER NINETEEN - YOU LOSE! WHAT'S NEXT?

Since your product is essentially weak, you're bound to hear these loathsome words, "Sorry Joe, but we're going to use someone else next month." Ouch! Actually, double ouch!! After all that work, which included treating your client like a king and through no fault of your own, you've been sent packing. Darn it! It happens to the best of us but it never stops hurting. The weaker the product, the more chance you have of hearing those words all too often. What do you do now?

First of all you must realize that their decision is not a reflection of you or your efforts. Don't take it personally! You probably kept them a lot longer than anyone else could have. After you have a good cry and get over being mad, map out your strategy to get back! What are you, nuts? Not at all. Why put all your efforts into gaining new clients when your old ones know you much better than they know your rivals? There's an obvious comfort zone that both the customer and you have attained. Milk it! Try to get anything you can to retain any contact. Most of the time because of your relationship you can always beg something, and if you're clever enough to come up with a daring new plan that is better than your competition's, you might just pull it off in a big way! Treat your old client as if he were a new business. You might surprise both them and yourself.

Once I lost an account and came up with an entirely new concept within an hour. My customer was surprised to say the least and exclaimed, "Why didn't you come up with this last month?" I explained that since I felt it wasn't broken, why fix it! He understood my position and gave me another shot after I asked him with the magic word - <u>please!</u> Actually, "pretty please with sugar on top". At this point it's always a good idea through proper questioning to ascertain exactly what the client needs from you. No sugar coating now! Black and white, what do you need from me? What do you expect? And what caused your dissatisfaction initially? Take notes in front of your customer and make sure everything goes perfectly. You're on borrowed time so be careful, and don't drop the ball again. Cover all your bases and you could salvage an account. But the point here is to not give up when you get the pink slip. Keep trying because you have a much better chance getting back someone that you know well than getting someone from a cold call. It's all in the numbers.

Remember, these rejections seem to go in streaks, and with a bad product, you might get a couple in a day. Now that's a bad day! But regardless of these setbacks, a great salesperson always remains optimistic. Now that's a tall order, indeed! Salespeople, who are around long enough, suffer their share of rebuffs, but an ultra-successful salesperson always maintains their dogged optimism. How do they do it?

First, they never take it personally as we've previously discussed. A weak salesperson will wonder abjectly "What did I do wrong? I must have said something stupid. I'm always messing things up. Why, why, why?" Notice the difference with the strong sales guru. He says, "their loss is my gain. Now I can concentrate on a larger account or a closer one!" Losers ponder what happened and continue to grouse about their losses. Winners hitch up their pants, take a deep breath, and go on to the next account, more determined than ever to sell a big one! Losses go with the territory. It hurts but don't let it get the best of you. The mind set needed in this type of situation is blatant <u>optimism.</u> Know that you will be successful, and you will be! Remember that list you made of clients who would order from a monkey if you weren't there? Go back to that and review each one of these and ask yourself why they like you so much. Write it out to drill it into your mind. I guarantee that after listing all your strong accounts and why they're so strong, you'll be on the road to forgetting all about your latest setback. And you know that's the point. It's a setback, not a defeat. Don't make a loss more important than it should be. On the road to success there are many setbacks and the champions use them as stepping stones rather than stumbling blocks. Some even go so far as to expect a certain amount of attrition. Maybe one a week, maybe one a month, but mark my words, it will happen. Now if you've been an industrious, hard working salesperson, you'll have plenty of prospects that will be ready to take the place of the one you've lost. That's why you keep working hard making new contacts and new customers. That's why when you lose one, you'll hardly notice!

Don't put all your eggs in one basket either. Diversify your business just like they do in the stock market. That way if one part of the market is doing better than another, you're covered. Big accounts,small ones, get them all! It's the best insurance policy for sales dominance you could ever have . Do you see how easy it is to cut your losses and accentuate the positives? Alas, you have to be half nuts to be good in sales. But the question is which half. The top, the bottom, the right side or left side? I don't know but we all have a crazy side and when you lose an account, plug into it. You'll need it and believe me when I tell you it will never let you down!

CHAPTER TWENTY - THE LAST WORD

I can't believe we're at the end already! Hasn't it been fun? I hope so because it's been a lot of fun and very instructional for me to write a book on this wonderful subject. You see, I appreciate Salespeople like no one else. Why? Because I am one! You are exceptional, don't forget it! Our vocation is special and should be viewed as such. It's a privilege to be able to make a living by talking and meeting others! Lots of people work very hard to eke out a meager subsistence that just barely pays the bills. My friends, we are at the zenith of living. If you looked at the recent Forbes 500 list of the Richest in America, Salesmen and Saleswomen were found throughout. We didn't have to go to school for 15 years to learn our trade, and we didn't have to be an apprentice hour after hour to learn our trade. We were born with it! However, it's not for everyone. You've either got it or you don't. But if you are fortunate enough to be graced with this unique talent, be thankful every day for it. Work hard! Don't be lazy. You have a chance that few have. Take full advantage of it! Don't squander your opportunity for success. It's a challenge. Don't be mislead. When you've sold more in an hour than most do in a year, keep going. If you've heard nothing but No's, and customers are dropping like flies, keep your chin up and above all, keep going. <u>You only lose if you quit!</u> Make up your mind that you're the Best Salesperson in the universe, and remember to keep this position you have to work hard! Nothing takes the place of hard work. Everything we've discussed in this primer has work as its theme. Doing that extra special something that separates you from the rest is how it's done.

I don't know how many friends and acquaintances have told me how lucky I am. How I have the Midas touch. But I'll tell you, the secret is hard work - not missing a trick! Go the extra mile and you'll be a winner. Guaranteed! It's really all in your hands. It's a numbers game that can be won only by dedication and perseverance.

The theme of this book has been how to sell something that doesn't work or isn't as good as the competitors. Ultimately now you know the answer, it's not the product, but the one who stands behind it! Remember if it was so easy there would be no need for Salespeople. If something was so good that it sold itself, your job would quickly disappear. People would phone in their orders and Operators would take the place of Salespeople. But realistically if you think all the tips in this book are only for those who sell an inferior product, you're wrong! <u>This book is for all Salespeople!</u> If these suggestions can help those whose product is weak, just think what it can do for you who have a good thing! Wow, it boggles the imagination to think what you could do with the mind set I've developed over the years selling a product that stinks. And you know what, I now sell something that's good! Can you believe it? After all these years I have something that is fairly easy to sell.

But did you notice I emphasized the words <u>mind set</u> or better yet gaining a <u>philosophy</u>. Really, that's what it takes to be successful, not memorizing scripts, or reacting a certain clever way to a sales-stopping statement. Develop yourself as a super Salesperson doing the extra things and walking the extra mile and in no time you could probably write a book yourself with all the great experiences you've had. At this point you will be the philosophy, instead of developing one! If you do that, you win!

But before I go back out to my territory to make a living, I wanted to make an offer to all you erstwhile salespeople out there! If you've come up with an absolute sales killer, one that you believe can't be overcome, fax it to me (510-829-6700) or send it by mail. I'll get you back an answer that will overcome any objection. Remember, I've never been stumped yet! And if you see me in person either addressing a group or just walking down the street, challenge me. I live for stuff like that. Hey, you bought my book. We're joined at the hip now. I'll be there for you! Remember you will succeed if you want it bad enough. I did!

Chapter 20

Happy trails and especially happy sales to all until we meet again...

ABOUT THE AUTHOR

How did he do it ?

- The youngest liquor store owner in California history, built sales from 0 to $1 million in record-setting time.

- Started a carpet cleaning company with no customers and built it to $1/2 million in sales.

- Became the #1 sales rep in the U.S. for a large corporation (over 75,000 employees) within just six months selling a product that just did not work! And then, believe it or not, kept all his customers for five years!

- Not satisfied, he was recruited for a start-up advertising publishing company and within three months their page count quadrupled, making it extremely attractive for a huge corporation to acquire it at a record breaking price!

Over 25 years of sales dominance from the front selling lines is now at your fingertips!!